RELIGIONS OF THE WORLD

I Am
Quaker

❖ FELICE BLANC ❖

The Rosen Publishing Group's
PowerKids Press™
New York

Published in 1999 by The Rosen Publishing Group, Inc.
29 East 21st Street, New York, NY 10010

First Edition

Book Design: Erin McKenna and Kim Sonsky

Photo Credits: p.4 © Mitch Diamond/International Stock; p. 7 © Art Resource; p. 8 © Baldwin H. Ward/Corbis-Bettmann; pp. 11, 12, 19 © Corbis-Bettman; p. 15 © Ryan Williams/International Stock; p. 16 © Bob Firth/International Stock; p. 20 © Scott Barrow/International Stock.

Blanc, Felice.
    I am Quaker / by Felice Blanc.
        p.   cm. — (Religions of the world)
    Includes index.
    Summary: A young Quaker explains the beliefs and practices of this religion.
    ISBN 0-8239-5264-9
    1. Society of Friends—Juvenile literature. [1. Society of Friends.] I. Title. Series: Religions of the world (Rosen Publishing Group)
    BX7731.2.B57 1996
    289.6—dc21   98-11796
                                                       CIP
                                                       AC

Manufactured in the United States of America

Contents

Serena

Hi! I'm Serena. My family lives in Harrisburg, Pennsylvania. We belong to a religious group called the Society of Friends. A **society** (so-SY-eh-tee) is a group of people who have something in common. We are known as friends, or Quakers. Some of the first Quakers often shook, or quaked, with **emotion** (e-MOH-shun) while they were praying. So people gave them the nickname Quakers.

◀ The Society of Friends includes people of all ages. They live all around the world.

5

Beginnings

The Society of Friends began in England in the seventeenth century. England was a **monarchy** (MON-ar-kee). That means the government was run by a king or queen. Back then, the king told the English people what they could and could not believe about God. But some people **rebelled** (re-BELD) against the king. They didn't want anyone telling them what to do. They wanted to decide things for themselves.

King James II was the monarch when George Fox started the Society of Friends. ▶

George Fox

In 1624, a boy named George Fox was born in England. As he grew older, he realized he was missing something in his life, but he didn't know what it was. He talked with ministers but they couldn't help him.

One day in 1646 he figured out what was wrong. He had been going to other people for help, but the answer was inside him. That answer was what Fox called the "Inner Light." He traveled around the country telling people about his **discovery** (dis-KUV-er-ee). Soon he had many followers.

◀ George Fox and his followers called themselves the Society of Friends.

The Light of God

George believed the Inner Light was in everyone, and that people would feel it if they worshiped God in silence. Friends are Christians, but they don't turn to a minister or priest to help them hear the words of God. Instead, God gives us the Inner Light so we can hear His words. The Inner Light is what helps us feel His **presence** (PREH-zents).

George started his Society in 1652. They believed they should always obey God first. Fox and many of the Friends were often put in jail for spreading their new religion.

Unlike other groups that punished people for questioning the rules, the Society of Friends ▶ thought questions were important.

Quaker Meetings

Quakers don't have church services. Instead, they have meetings. These meetings are usually held without a minister or other leader. They take place once a week and last about an hour.

In meeting, everyone sits in silence. They wait to **sense** (SENS) the Inner Light of God inside them. When they do, they may stand up and say whatever they feel. Sometimes the whole hour goes by without anyone speaking.

◄ At a Quaker meeting, Friends speak when they feel God speaking to them.

Some Differences

Meetings that don't have a leader are called **unprogrammed** (un-PROH-gramd) meetings. But not every Quaker goes to this kind of meeting. Early in this century, some Quakers decided they didn't agree with the unprogrammed meetings. Instead, they began their own programmed meetings. These meetings are much more like other Christian services. One person leads everyone else in prayer and sometimes in songs and Bible readings.

Some programmed Quaker meetings take place in meetinghouses that look like traditional Christian churches. ▶

A Simple Life

One thing that Quakers agree on is the importance of living a simple life. For example, many Quakers don't buy fancy clothes, jewelry, or extra cars. Most Quaker meetings are held in a plain, small building. This place is called a meetinghouse. Unlike many churches and temples, meetinghouses don't have colorful stained-glass windows, statues, or paintings.

◀ Quakers may live in very simple houses, such as this one.

Everyone's Equal

Quakers believe that everyone is equal. Friends help people who aren't being treated fairly by others.

Many years ago, Quakers often helped the Native Americans when other people did not. Quakers were also against **slavery** (SLAY-ver-ee). Some Friends helped southern slaves escape to freedom.

Quakers were some of the first to demand equal rights for women. Quakers still try to help people all over the world who are fighting for equal rights.

The Quakers always treated Native Americans with respect. ▶

Choose Peace, Not War

One of the most important Quaker beliefs is **pacifism** (PASS-if-izm). We believe that because all people are created equal, we should love everyone, even our enemies. Quakers never **participate** (par-TIH-si-payt) in war. Instead, during wartime Quakers have helped by taking care of soldiers and other people who are hurt. Quakers have even gone to jail because they've refused to fight.

Quakers are known for solving problems fairly and peacefully.

I Am Quaker

Quakers don't agree on everything. We live all around the world, and have different ideas about what it means to be a Friend. Some pray in different ways. Some wear very plain clothes and others (like me!) wear bright colors. That's okay. We know that one of the reasons George Fox founded the Society of Friends was so that people could feel the Inner Light and have the freedom to figure things out on their own.

Glossary

discovery (dis-KUV-er-ee) Something that has been found for the first time.

emotion (e-MOH-shun) A strong feeling, such as anger or sadness.

monarchy (MON-ar-kee) A government headed by a king or queen.

pacifism (PASS-if-izm) Choosing not to use war or violence to solve problems.

participate (par-TIH-si-payt) To take part in something.

presence (PREH-zents) The act of something being there.

rebel (re-BEL) To go against the rules.

sense (SENS) To be aware of something.

slavery (SLAY-ver-ee) The system of one person "owning" another.

society (so-SY-eh-tee) A group of people who have something in common.

unprogrammed (un–PROH-gramd) Without a plan or leader.

Index